RENDEZVOUS

Reliving the Fur Trade Era
—1825 to 1840—

RENDEZVOUS

Reliving the Fur Trade Era
—1825 to 1840—

Text and Photographs

by

Kurt Rhody

Kurt R. Rhody (signature)

Foreword by Ray Glazner

Rob Reilly, Editor

SIERRA PRESS, INC.
Mariposa, CA

Dedication

This book is a visual tribute to Buckskinners past, present and
future. And to everyone I encountered while working on it.
Without their assistance and cooperation this book would not
have been possible. Also to my mom and dad who have always
encouraged me. Thank you all!

ISBN 0-939365-49-9

Copyright 1996 by Sierra Press, Inc.
4988 Gold Leaf Drive
Mariposa, CA 95338

First Printing: Spring 1996.

Table of Contents

Foreword
by Ray Glazner

Through the hazy smoke of campfires one sees a primitive campsite, replete with figures dressed in clothing styles dating back 150 to 200 years. Is it a dream? Have we entered a time warp? Neither—people are simply enjoying themselves at a modern rendezvous. For these participants, or visitors who happen by, the clock has been turned back to the early 1800s.

The current rendezvous is a reenactment of Fur Trade Era get-togethers when trappers, hunters, Indians, traders and their families met to exchange goods and services vis-a-vis the early trade fairs. These fairs have been held from the middle ages to the present in both Europe and America.

Today's reenactors try to emulate that period of American history when furs were traded for manufactured goods. This practice of trading goods for furs is, in many respects, the story of the exploration and settlement of America. Having found no gold or silver in eastern North America, the European explorers relied instead on the rich land, seemingly inexhaustable timber resources and an abundance of fur-bearing animals. Fur pelts were used in the process of making hats—no self-respecting adult would be seen in public bare-headed—and the unique fur from the beaver made the best felt for hats. Native Indians had the ability to trap animals and found the newcomers more than willing to trade their manufactured goods (hatchets, pots, tools, beads, cloth, etc.) for furs.

The major European powers vied with one another for control of native tribes and territory—and the natural resources therein. After eliminating their Dutch, Swedish, Russian and French competitors, control eventually came down to the English and American settlers.

At first, trading was conducted at forts and towns on the frontier. By the early 1800s, however, the frontier was so far removed from the forts that it took too long to travel through the wilderness, and back, to be practical. As a consequence, from 1825 to 1840, the main fur trading was done at an annual Rendezvous in the Rocky Mountains. Traders with goods would leave St. Louis, Missouri, in the spring and meet the Indians and fur trappers at a predesignated site in July. Furs and trading goods would change hands, inevitably followed by a rather raucous party thrown by the trading partners!

Today's reenacters try to recreate both the look and the feel of those early camps. People come from all over the world and from all walks of life to recreate those colorful and exciting days. For participants, the rendezvous has evolved into a unique way to "step back in time" and enjoy an outdoor event in learning, teaching and appreciating an avocation that is based upon living history.

The images and essays in this book provide the reader a glimpse of what life was like for our Fur Trade Era ancestors, as well as what today's reenactors enjoy as a fun and growing hobby.

Contemporary participants ("Buckskinners") reenact the
18th and 19th century's tempestuous interaction of
American Indians, trappers and mountain men.

RENDEZVOUS

Reliving the Fur Trade Era
—1825 to 1840—

by

Kurt Rhody

Spirit of the Past

The word "rendezvous" was first used to describe the 18th century's tempestuous interaction among American Indians, trappers and mountain men in the 1760s. At a French fort that had fallen to the English during the seven-year French and Indian War, a young English captain by the name of Smith wrote a letter to his superior in Detroit saying, "If I do not have supplies when the trappers, mountain men and Indians return in the spring, they will tear the fort apart." He got his supplies and a peaceable "rendezvous" ensued.

American farmers and villagers of the early-19th century trapped fur-bearing game as a way to supplement their meager coffers (when they were unable to till the soil). This required trekking across the wide-open expanses of the midwestern wilderness. So great was this expanse that it was not uncommon for these excursions to last from a few months to up to a year. Most, upon their return to "civilization," sold their furs in St. Louis, Missouri, a growing hub of commerce situated on the western frontier. But to go farther west, beyond the Rocky Mountains, required another strategy. It took too long to get there and back to make it profitable for individual trappers. So fur companies hired trappers to stay out one to two years, resupplying them during the summer. These summer get-togethers are known today as the Rocky Mountain Rendezvous.

Although "rendezvous" were a part of the American landscape for two centuries (from 1640 to 1840), today, the term is most commonly used in reference to the Rocky Mountain Rendezvous, which only lasted from 1825 to 1840. This was, in fact, the final chapter of the Fur Trade Era in American history.

The first Rocky Mountain Rendezvous was organized by William H. Ashley in 1825. He was not a mountain man but, rather, a shrewd businessman whose goal was to make his fortune in fur trading. Ashley's idea was innovative and bold. He would hire a hundred trappers and outfit them—in return for half the beaver they trapped.

Ashley's men headed up the Missouri River, where they divided into small groups, and proceeded to trap. Telling the men to meet him at Henrys Fork, Wyoming, later that summer, Ashley returned to St. Louis to gather supplies. And so, the site of the first Rocky Mountain Rendezvous was selected. After re-supplying that summer at Henrys Fork, fur traders and trappers agreed on a locale for their next gathering.

At these first rendezvous, the men swapped tales of their adventures, drank large quantities of whiskey, gambled and brawled. However, their main reason for coming together was to exchange goods. The trappers needed traps, guns, gunpowder, flour and other domestic necessities. In return, the traders wanted beaver pelts to ship to the eastern United States and England, where they would be fashioned into hats that were popular in Europe at the time.

The Rocky Mountain Rendezvous era lasted only 16 years, but it was a time of historic discovery and legendary adventure. The men were strong, boisterous, colorful and proud—some larger than life. Men like Kit Carson and Jedediah Smith were among those who regularly attended rendezvous, with Indians accounting for almost half the participants during the get-togethers. Friendly Indians, such as the Crow, traded or gambled everything from clothing to themselves!

The Indian tribesmen taught mountain men how to live off the land, what plants to eat, how to prepare them, and how to track game. Without their help, the trappers would have been far less able to endure the hardships of an

unforgiving wilderness. Many mountain men ultimately married Native American women, since few white women were willing to endure the mountain man's lifestyle.

During the winter months, when streams froze over and men could no longer trap beaver, they either stayed in a frontier town or lived with friendly Indians for the season. Some formed groups and built cabins in which to ride out the harsh winters. Still others lived on their own, depending on the availability of food in their locales.

After the last rendezvous (in 1840) at Green River, Wyoming, some mountain men continued to trap, others became guides, and still others tried to adapt to civilization again. The "mountain man" endured 200 years before disappearing into the fabric of American history. Although the Fur Trade Era is over, the spirit of camaraderie is alive and well at today's reenacted rendezvous.

Those who participate in the reenactment of Fur Trade Era rendezvous find themselves immersed in an age of discovery in American history. Attired in painstakingly recreated, authentic period dress, they relive the legends told nightly in the warm glow of communal campfires. The smiling faces and colorful characters found at contemporary rendezvous are a reminder of a time and lifestyle far different from that most of us live in the late-20th century.

The spirit of friendly competition found at modern
rendezvous mirrors that of the 19th century. The original
attendees considered the Rocky Mountain Rendezvous to be
a great opportunity to compete in a number of competitive
skills. Knife and tomahawk throwing and target shooting
were important tests of survival skills trappers needed in
the wilderness. These contests, as well as horseback riding
and survival skills, are reenacted today.

Music allowed mountain men to reconnect with their heritage. Spending prolonged periods alone in the wilderness gave trappers ample time to hone their skills. The sounds of music—from impromptu flute recitals along Traders Row to the chords of a guitarist practicing prior to an evening performance—are among the many joys sure to bring smiles to the faces of modern rendezvousers, or "Buckskinners," as they refer to themselves.

Fur Trade Era merchants set up a Traders Row, where trappers could acquire tools, lead for shot, candles, bolts of cloth, liquor (always a favorite) and perhaps a new gun. The trader seen here is displaying a "blunder-buster." Not of much use for hunting, this weapon was typically used by guards at forts, and on ships and stagecoaches. The blunder-buster was designed for easy loading and intimidation.

Tools of Yesteryear

Today, late in the 20th century, most of our tools are made by machine. During the Fur Trade Era (the 18th and 19th centuries) tools were made by hand. Hands were the ultimate "tool" trappers possessed. Tools of the mountain man were not tools of convenience—they were tools of survival. Whether a pack animal carried most of their supplies, or they carried everything on their backs in a wood-framed pack (often weighing 80 lbs or more), they carried few luxuries in those days. Because the mountain man was so limited in what he could carry, the tools he used had to be job-specific, well constructed, and able to withstand the harshness of the environment. If a man's gun malfunctioned in the wilderness and he was unable to fix it, he might not survive.

All tools played an important role in the Fur Trade Era. One depended on them for travel, protection, cooking and many other facets of daily existence. At rendezvous, among the many traders, a blacksmith could usually be found. He made everything from candlestick holders and cooking utensils to horseshoes. Mountain men would tell him what they needed and he custom-made the requested items.

The trap was the primary work tool of the mountain man. It was hand-made and most trappers carried anywhere from six to twelve of them. Knives of assorted shapes and sizes, horse tack and guns (either rifle or smooth-bore) were also standard tools.

Trappers did not use their guns often, since the sound would attract Indians in the vicinity. To hunt game, they often set snares or other types of traps. On those occasions when a gun was used, the hunter would remove the bullet from the animal. After five or six spent bullets were collected, they would be re-melted in order to mold new ones. In this way, the trapper did not have to pack as much lead, thus reducing the overall pack weight. Other items in the pack usually included an ax or tomahawk, a "house wife" (sewing kit), compass, flints to make fire, and lead and molds to make bullets.

Game served as both food and "tool." Hides were used for clothing, blankets and (in the case of big game animals such as the buffalo) they could also be used to make a tipi or a "bowl" boat. A "bowl" boat was made by fastening reeds together in a circular shape, with the hide stretched over the configuration. The trapper put his belongings (including his clothes) into the bowl boat for fording rivers and streams, getting only his body wet. Traversing rapids could be especially hazardous, if the bowl boat capsized in the turbulent waters, he could lose everything.

In addition to the hide, animal bones were used as handles for tools, buttons on clothing and as jewelry worn around the neck. Claws and teeth served as personal decoration and leg tendons were used as thread (sinew) for leather working.

Like their ancestors, the "Buckskinners" (as today's rendezvousers call themselves) take great pride in handcrafting each tool as if their very survival depended on it. No detail is too small in striving for authenticity in recreating the tools of yesteryear's mountain man. Today we are surrounded by tools (of convenience) from the time we wake up until the time we retire at night—often forgetting how important tools are in our daily lives.

Webster's dictionary describes "tool" as "an instrument . . . used or worked by hand." Living in an era when people made most of what they needed by hand, the mountain man probably considered his hands to be his most valuable tool.

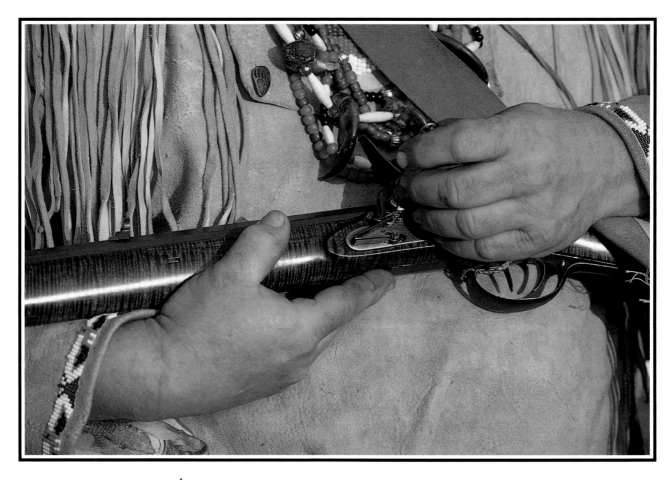

As anyone who works with their hands will tell you, a good tool is like a good friend—reliable, trustworthy and lifelong. The J and S Hawkins rifle shown here would have been worth its weight in gold to its proud owner. Knives, such as the "Damascus" style seen here, were meticulously hand-crafted using two metal layers, one hard and one soft, that were pounded together and folded over themselves at least 800 times before being welded together. The knife's surface was acid-etched, thereby revealing a kaleidoscope of colors found in the steel. The 4-string dulcimer shown here was a popular 18th century instrument that pre-dates both the guitar and the banjo.

Pack animals were a necessity for many trappers. The horse was a moving van, storage facility—and friend. The use of wheeled handcarts, while not practical in the wilds of the 19th century, is a popular method of transporting personal belongings at modern rendezvous, where motorized vehicles are prohibited. Of the many skills necessary for survival in the wilderness, perhaps none is so important as the mastery of fire. To survive, the mountain man learned several ways of starting a fire. Without fire he could not cook, melt lead for molding shot, smoke jerky or, most important, survive the bitter cold encountered in the Rocky Mountains.

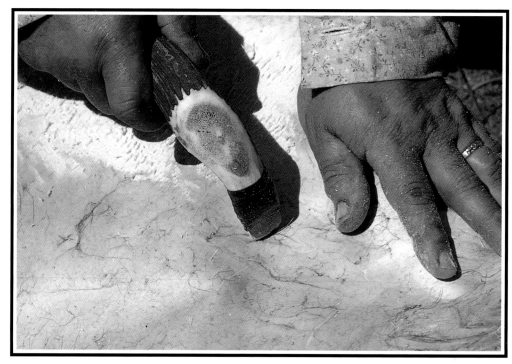

Fur Trade Era trappers fashioned many goods from the materials they found in the wilderness. They learned to use many parts of the animals they hunted. Bones and antlers were carved into tools and jewelry, hides were tanned and fashioned into clothes using the animal's tendons (sinew) as thread. Natural plant products (such as gourds) could be emptied, dried and used as canteens. Plant fibers could be spun into rope or string and used to secure the trapper's pelts to his pack animal. Many of these skills were learned from the Native Americans who called the same mountains home for centuries prior to the arrival of 18th and 19th century trappers.

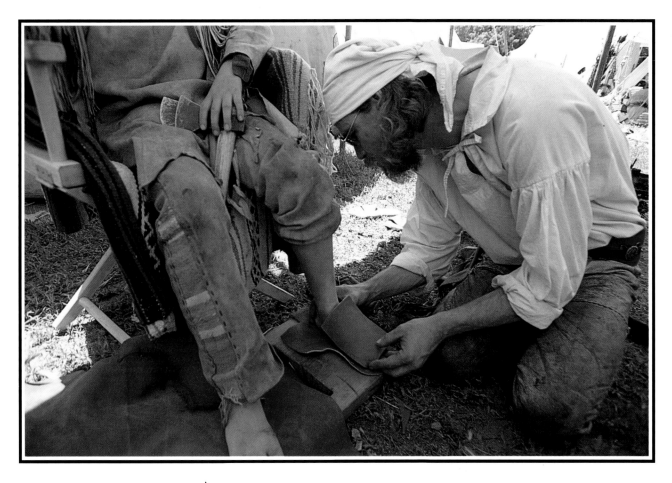

As self-sufficient as the mountain man was, there were certain items that could only be acquired at the annual rendezvous. Among the most important traders found at rendezvous was the blacksmith. Kitchen utensils, knives, molds for pouring lead and, especially, traps were some of the goods the blacksmith made to order or had on hand at rendezvous. Although many trappers were adept at making their own footware from the animals they hunted and trapped, today's Buckskinners often rely on rendezvous craftsmen to fashion their hand-made footwear.

In experienced, talented hands, the tools crafted for survival can become pieces of art. Remarkably intricate designs in the stock of a rifle, the simplicity of form-following-function in the blacksmith's tent and the perfection of proportion found in a hand-carved gun stock—all raise the commonplace to the level of art through personal expression. Contemporary Buckskinners have been responsible for making certain these artforms are not lost in an age when we rely heavily on mass-produced goods.

Friends and Family

ountain men, trappers, Native Americans and traders were the sole participants of the Rocky Mountain Rendezvous. That tradition has evolved. The typical rendezvous of the late-20th century has a strong family presence—from infants to grandparents.

People now rendezvous for many reasons, but one common thread is a determination to escape the urban wilderness and get back in touch with nature. Buckskinners also have a passion for American history—a book or television program does not suffice—they want to relive it. Rendezvousing is hard work. Setting up camp can take up to half a day, depending on the complexity of the camp and number of people helping. Many comforts that we enjoy in everyday life are prohibited at these events—ice cubes, flashlights and flush toilets to name a few. Jeans, T-shirts and tennis shoes are replaced at rendezvous by a style that more closely resembles that of Davy Crockett, Daniel Boone and Nattie Bumpo. Buckskinners rendezvous because they do not want to forget a colorful part of the American past.

One of the major benefits for Buckskinner parents is that their kids are not sitting in classrooms learning about American history through books—they are actually living it. Children live their heritage, wearing authentic Fur Trade Era clothing and accessories, right down to the moccasins on their feet.

Children at rendezvous encampments learn the art of conversation while sitting around a campfire at night—without the distractions of television or computer games. "It's hard for them at first, but they soon get the hang of it," says a father of two. They are taught a different set of values—learning to entertain themselves and relate to other people.

Camp children learn to weave baskets, make leather products and do bead work. They learn how to throw a tomahawk, sharpen knives and other survival skills a young person would be expected to know growing up in the Fur Trade Era. At night, kids go on snipe hunts or sit around the campfire singing songs, playing games and retelling stories about their ancestors.

Many of the early mountain men were outlaws who seldom used their real names—taking colorful nicknames instead. Continuing this tradition today, many Buckskinners have "camp names." A camp name is like an Indian name, it is given in remembrance of a particular event or to accentuate a personal character trait. As a Buckskinner, you do not choose a name such as "Tree Killer," "Crazy George" or "Stargazer," you earn it!

What keeps Buckskinners coming back to rendezvous time and again are the people. "Possum" has been attending rendezvous for years, mostly with the same people, and yet he has no idea what they do in real life. You do not talk about things like that, it just doesn't matter. This tacit respect and acceptance creates a bond between people—you can meet someone for the first time and feel you have known them all your life.

People attracted to rendezvous include bankers, doctors, government employees, corporate CEOs and social nomads. But at rendezvous none of that matters, there are no class divisions. Here, everyone is considered an equal.

For children, rendezvous is a time of blissful joy. The simplicity of camp life provides youngsters with ample time to play, explore, discover and learn about themselves and the natural world around them.

Contemporary rendezvous is not only about the present reliving the past, it is also about the present teaching the future. Participants range in age from infants to grandparents—with many teaching and all learning the art of living.

While families may not have played an important role at Fur Trade
Era rendezvous, they are central to contemporary reenactments. The
cynicism of contemporary society is tempered by the generosity of
spirit found at today's rendezvous. Hugs from elders and children,
smiling faces at the dinner table, a child taking a "bucket-bath"—all
are indicative of the spirit of joy and sharing found at rendezvous.

One of the greatest pleasures of rendezvous is that of neighbor helping neighbor. Strangers become friends over a cup of coffee or tea. At rendezvous people concentrate on what they all have in common and do not allow petty differences to interfere with the enjoyment of life. For many mountain men the time spent in the wilderness was shared with a pet, which was sometimes the only familiar face they would see for months at a time. Dogs, in addition to their skills at trailing game and providing security around camp, were also close emotional companions in the wilderness—companions who demanded little but gave much.

W*hen people think of the quintessential mountain man, they envision men with beards—as Hollywood has portrayed them in most movies with Fur Trade Era themes. In fact, many were clean-shaven, especially those who wintered with Native Americans who did not care for beards or facial hair of any kind.*

Home Sweet Home

The shelter of choice for most Buckskinners is either the tipi or a canvas tent (in a variety of styles). The tipi, a Sioux word meaning "used for dwelling," was borrowed from the Plains Indians. The graceful shape and historical familiarity of the tipi makes it a popular shelter at today's rendezvous. It is also noted for its durability and adaptability in adverse weather conditions.

Tipi poles were usually made of pine, cedar, or spruce. Flexible tree woods were not used for these poles. A liner (or dew cloth) was placed inside the tipi. This cloth prevented dew from collecting on the inside walls. In addition, with a liner in place an enemy could not shoot at one's shadow on an illuminated tipi wall.

Another popular shelter was the wall tent, a style preferred by traders and the military. Its four sides hang rigidly straight—not unlike the walls of a house.

Today's Buckskinners cook with the same tools our ancestors used, including iron pots suspended over open fires, iron skillets and Dutch ovens. The Dutch oven is an iron pot that has a "rimmed" iron lid—thus, coals can be put on top of the "oven" as well as beneath. The design of the lid prevents the coals from rolling off. The advantage of such an "oven" is that the food is cooked evenly, top to bottom. In mastering the Dutch oven, patience, skill and an affinity for trial and error is required. You learn quickly that some foods require eight coals on the bottom and four on the top with a cooking period of so many minutes—it varies from dish to dish. In experienced hands, anything from fresh bread to peach cobbler can be cooked in a Dutch oven.

In contrast, a typical cook kit carried by 19th century mountain men consisted of a tin cup (with lid) and an iron skillet which had an opening for a handle. This portable skillet kept overall pack weight down. The trappers' diet was high in protein, featuring venison or other game meat, as well as in-season grains. Some of their carbohydrates came from "boden." A popular foodstuff, boden is the contents of a buffalo's intestines (such as dried grass) which provides a rich source of vitamins and carbohydrates. A typical dinner might include stew with vegetables dug from the ground, biscuits and a favorite spirit.

Contemporary Buckskinners use the same methods to start a fire as did the early mountain men. Fire was one of the basic "tools" of survival. A common way to start a fire was by using flint and steel. A spark produced by striking flint and steel was directed into a piece of punk wood (from a dead pine tree), dry grass, or charred linen. The ember was then carefully blown until it produced a small flame.

Another fire-starting approach was using a flintlock. The trapper removed the lock from the gun, placed tinder (instead of gunpowder) in the frizzen (powder chamber), pulled the trigger back to full cock and fired, sending sparks into the tinder. He also learned from the Indians how to use a bow-and-board, achieving fire by friction.

In addition to cooking and providing heat, the camp's firepit is a natural gathering place to talk about the day's events, work on craft projects, mend torn or ripped clothing, sharpen knives, or clean guns. The firepit was, and still is, an important center for socializing.

This socializing almost always includes the exchange of information, ideas and skills. You may start out with one or two people sitting around camp under a cool blue sky talking about bead work. Before you know it, you

are no longer talking about it, but are demonstrating to one another the hands-on techniques! At night the camp remains alive. Campfires glitter like gold under the evening sky. Candle lanterns swing from side to side as people circulate, sprinkling the darkness like fireflies. As fires glow, Buckskinners (wrapped in their warm, blanket-like kapotes) spend pleasant hours with neighbors and friends.

Most mountain men did not own elaborate shelters. A simple one-pole (or hunting) tent was often the most practical shelter available. A small tent or "lean-to," constructed of materials found around camp, was often the only shelter available for use during inclement weather.

One of the most popular shelters used by modern Buck-skinners is the "wall tent." This vertically-walled shelter was popular with traders at the original rendezvous because of its interior space, assuming the means of transporting it were available. The tipi is another popular shelter at today's reenactments. Its use by Native Americans (who also attended the Rocky Mountain Rendezvous in significant numbers) make its use at modern encampments historically accurate—not to mention fun!

The fragrance of wood smoke filled the air of Fur Trade Era
rendezvous just as it does at today's reenactments. Whether it's from
a small, personal fire to grill a venison steak or a bonfire to light up
the night, the aromas of juniper, oak and pine permeate the atmo-
sphere at rendezvous. Today's Buckskinners cook with the same style
pots, pans, skillets and Dutch ovens their predecessors used.
Mountain men served their meals (if at all) on plates or in bowls
made of wood, tin or pewter. Silver dinnerware was available, but
was used primarily by the affluent.

Mountain men and trappers learned to make use of many of the plants growing in their immediate environment. They often learned from Native Americans which seeds, fruits, mushrooms, bulbs and grains were safe, and how to prepare them. Buckskinners still enjoy taking the time to grind their own corn to make flour. The evocative fragrance of baking biscuits wafting through camp is a reward well worth the effort!

While elaborate kitchen set-ups were not practical for the 19th century mountain man in the wilderness, many contemporary Buckskinners choose to differ. Home is, after all, where meals are prepared—and at rendezvous, no one goes hungry. Authentic 19th century meals are the normal fare and you are always welcome to pull up a chair, or log. Many Buckskinners consider the 5 p.m. "camp meeting" important enough to forego a delectable evening meal.

The trappers of the 19th century spent prolonged periods in solitude. This time was filled with tending traps, tracking game and tanning hides, as well as the daily chores of mending clothes, cleaning tools and repairing traps. What time was left for other pursuits may have been spent playing a musical instrument, reading a good book or adding decorative adornments to clothing. The "fringe" often seen on the pants, shirts and coats of mountain men was commonly used as string to tie objects or to carry beads. Such utilitarianism is consistent with a life lived in the wilderness, where simplicity is part of survival.

Personal Style

When winter tightened its grip on the land, some mountain men learned to read. Others spent this "shelter time" making new tools and repairing old ones. The mountain man lived a simple existence. To eliminate boredom during the long months of winter, some spent the time personalizing their belongings. This included scrimshaw work on powder horns, decorating buckskins and doing small crafts. Even with all this time on his hands, he would not undertake larger projects, such as furniture-building, because he could not take it with him in the spring.

Some of the styles and fashions the mountain man favored came from Native Americans, like the moccasins he wore or adding fringe to his buckskins. He also adopted the materials, designs and intricate patterns found in Indian clothing. Some trappers spent countless winter hours decorating everything with beads, from moccasins to shirts. European glass beads, called chevrons because of the v-shaped pattern visible in them, were highly prized for their color and brilliance.

Although modern clothing styles are more under-stated than that of our Fur Trade ancestors, style was as important then as it is today. A mountain man's clothing was often adapted from the styles of the Indians around him. If he married a squaw, she inherited the job of designing and mending his clothes. Environment also dictated his style. He learned what was practical to wear, such as an animal skin cap to keep his head dry and warm in rain or snow. It also provided him with a degree of camouflage in the wilderness.

Something as seemingly mundane as a tote bag made of elk, buffalo, or deer hide might be adorned with brightly colored beads and finished using a fox's (or other small animal's) head for the cover. Today, the same bag would most likely be made of cowhide, adorned with patterns etched into the leather.

Next to his traps, the mountain man's gun was his most highly prized possession. Some of these guns were adorned with decorative patterns carved into the wood stock, with the exposed metal parts often being etched in an intricate style. He did not own much, but what he had was treasured and protected.

This emphasis on personal style is one of the ingredients that makes today's rendezvous so exciting to attend. From the moment you arrive at rendezvous, the first thing that catches your attention is the way people are dressed. As you walk down Traders Row, you feel as if you had walked through a portal into the past. The sound of gunfire is heard in the distance. Out of the corner of your eye you see a blacksmith sweating over a piece of red-hot metal. From behind, a boy pulling a cart passes you. The aroma of baking bread floats in the air like mist rising from the ground.

Many Buckskinners undertake extensive research into the styles and techniques used by our ancestors during the Fur Trade Era, demonstrating how much they care about preserving our past—both culturally and artistically. The sounds, sights and very tastes of a bygone era are recreated by today's Buckskinners, who refuse to let its memory die.

Buckskinners take great pride in how they adorn themselves. The creation of clothes and jewelry is an expression of personality, and the choice of materials found in the natural world provides unlimited possibilities. Many Buckskinners choose to use bone, antler, leather, fur and even rattlesnake rattles to make a statement about themselves and their skills.

Hand-made clothes were a part of the mountain man's life—usually made from the materials at hand, such as leather. Traders brought bolts of cloth with them to the Rocky Mountain Rendezvous, from which light-weight clothes could be crafted. Today's Buckskinners use the same materials to hand-craft their clothes. The style of clothing selected says much about the wearer and basic materials are often crafted into elegant apparel.

Leather, which was available to the mountain man on a regular basis, was put to virtually every use imaginable. When properly brain-tanned, it was soft and supple and could be fashioned into shirts, pants, coats, hats, belts, shoes and bags. The finishing touch might be beads or bones—or even the head of a fox! As modern as dark glasses appear, they were used by 19th century mountain men—especially at high elevations. They were, and still are, available in blue, green and clear. The brown-ish-yellow that was available in the 19th century is no longer made because of the toxic chemicals required to produce the color.

Proper headware was a necessity for Fur Trade Era mountain men. During cold weather the human body loses a tremendous amount of heat from the head—and a fur-covered hat was an invaluable survival tool. Today's Buckskinner often chooses a style of hat worn by early settlers—including the English, French, Russians, Germans, Swedes and Dutch.

The selection of clothing made by the modern
Buckskinner is entirely personal. Some choose
to outfit themselves head-to-toe in tanned
leather, which can be darkened to personal taste
by holding it in the smoke of a smoldering fire.
The longer it's over the fire, the darker it
becomes. This process also affords a degree of
"water-proofing," as oils in the smoke penetrate
and seal the porous leather. Others choose
styles more typical of traders, who were able to
wear store-bought fashions. Still others opt for
the colorful wardrobes of Native Americans.

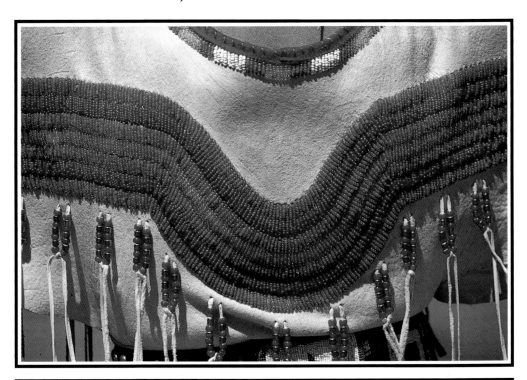

The influence of Native Americans is obvious in the jewelry worn by 19th century mountain men and 20th century Buckskinners. The glass beads brought to America by European settlers were also known as "trading beads" because they were prized by Native Americans. Tribesmen showed the mountain men how to use these colorful "new" objects in combination with traditional materials (like bone and leather) to create clothes and jewelry still admired and considered fashionable today.

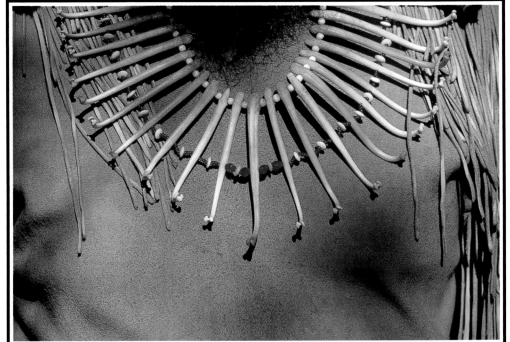

Days of Rendezvous

How do contemporary and historic rendezvous compare? The original Rocky Mountain Rendezvous were held for conducting business, gambling, drinking and replenishing stocks to carry on one's livelihood. The mountain man was a loner. He was concerned about how much money he was going to make and whether he could, or could not, locate beaver. Today we still trade and replenish our stocks, but it is a lifestyle that Buckskinners are recreating, with a strong emphasis on family values.

The modern rendezvous was initiated in the mid-1950s by a group of recreationists in Ohio, followed closely by another group in Indiana—where the National Muzzle Loading Rifle Association had been conducting shooting competitions since the 1930s. There was no attempt to reenact the living history aspects of the Fur Trade Era in the early days. The first National Rendezvous was the "Western" held in the early 1970s in Nebraska. Since then, the number of events has increased to nine National Rendezvous a year, plus thousands of smaller regional, or local, events. Nationwide, more than 80,000 Buckskinners rendezvous annually.

Contemporary rendezvous are family-oriented. There is a spirit of teaching, learning and togetherness among participants. Parents feel at ease letting their kids out of sight for hours at a time because rendezvous are usually held in out-of-the-way locales. There are no intersections or cars driving by at high speeds to worry about, and you are rendezvousing with people of high moral and ethical standards.

Pilgrims (newcomers) just beginning to rendezvous may not realize that camp children are being watched by others. A trader comments, "You have something in common and everyone is there for the same reason you are. We take care of and respect one another." People feel a sense of community. "Do unto others" is the Golden Rule at rendezvous encampments. Modern-day Buckskinners know they have a stake and say in what happens—and that is their strength. Such traits as honesty, trust and respect are not simply encouraged—they are expected. Camp justice is essentially black and white, with few shades of gray.

There are many reasons why people rendezvous today. One young girl explains, "I feel welcome walking into anyone's camp and sitting down and starting up a conversation." An elderly man adds, "It's the people that bring me back year after year." And a mother concludes, "I like the social values that are passed on to the kids."

For children, and adults, there are classes and seminars to attend. If you have a particular handicraft interest, someone probably teaches a class in it at rendezvous. You can learn everything from how to make medicines from the plants around you to forging metal. For those of a more competitive nature, there are contests in everything from target shooting and horseback riding, to tomahawk throwing and survival skills.

For most Buckskinners, rendezvous is the celebration of recreating a way of life worth preserving . . . and the satisfaction of knowing that it is still possible, at the end of the 20th century, to live in harmony with nature.

Two young girls gleefully dance across a sun-washed
summer meadow to the sounds of banjo, fiddle and guitar.
Is it any wonder that so many find the modern rendezvous
so much fun?

Swapping tall-tales, laughing, joking and playing games
are as much a part of today's rendezvous as they were of
the Fur Trade Era. Whether bathed in the glow of a
campfire or gingerly sipping the morning's first cup of
coffee, Buckskinners learn about themselves as they enjoy
the company of others.

Traders Row is the place for conducting business at rendezvous. Many of the hand-made tools used by our ancestors are no longer found in contemporary life, or have simply been replaced by more convenient forms. It is on Traders Row that modern mountain men and women find those items that connect them to their heritage. The level of trust between trader and Buckskinner is evidenced by traders leaving their booths unattended—asking only that the shopper leave the right amount for their purchase!

The spirit of competition that was so much a part of Fur Trade Era rendezvous is still alive and well. In addition to various "target" competitions, there are any number of games in which Buckskinners participate. Shown here is a Native American game similar to lacrosse. Two weighted bags, connected by a rope, must be thrown, using only a stick, through two goalposts. Those too young, or old, to play a game requiring such physical prowess, watch from the sidelines.

Visitors to Buckskinner encampments cannot help but notice that it seems everyone is doing something with their hands. Reenacting a period of history when virtually everything was hand-made keeps these people busy. Cleaning and adjusting guns, making jewelry and leather goods, and learning to carve and form a "ku" stick are regular activities. Informal classes led by experienced Buckskinners are held regularly. Leather working, jewelry making, plant identification, wilderness survival skills and tracking game are among the subjects shared.

One of the most colorful events at rendezvous is the "camp
meeting." Participants gather late in the day to discuss any
number of issues that may have come up. The "Bushway"
(master-at-arms) is in charge and he mediates and settles
differences between campers. The final camp meeting is a
celebration in which most Buckskinners participate. All depart
the encampment with a sense of satisfaction and anticipation—
looking forward to the next scheduled rendezvous!

About the Photographs

All photographs in this book were made with a Canon EOS-1, using lenses of from 20mm to 300mm. All exposures were made on Fuji films (Fujichrome 100, Velvia and Provia) and were hand-held. Aperture and shutter-speeds were not recorded.

Suggested Reading

Churchill, E. James. *The Complete Book of Tanning of Skins and Furs.* Mechanicsburg, PA: Stack Pole Publishing Co. 1983.

Clark, Wm. and Lewis, Meriwether. *The History of the Lewis and Clark Expedition, Volumes 1-3.* (1893). Reprint. New York, NY: Dover Publications.

DeVoto, Bernard. *Across the Wide Missouri.* (1947). Reprint. Boston, MA: Houghton Mifflin Co. 1975.

DeVoto, Bernard (Editor). *The Journals of Lewis and Clark.* (1953). Reprint. Boston, MA: Houghton Mifflin Co.

Morgan, L. Dale. *Jedediah Smith.* Lincoln, NE: Univ. of Nebraska Press. 1964.

Russell, Osborne. *Journal of a Trapper.* Lincoln, NE: Univ. of Nebraska Press. 1964.

Schroen, Karl. *The Forged Knife.* Knoxville, TN: Knife World Publishing Co. 1984.

Scurlock, H. William (Editor). *Book of Buckskinning, Volumes 1-7.* Texarkana, TX: Rebel Publishing Co. 1981-1995.

Spring, Ted. *Sketch Books, Volumes 1-10.* Osseo, MN: Track of the Wolf Co. 1986-1995.

Stone, Irving. *Men To Match My Mountains.* (1956) Reprint. New York, NY: Berkley Publishing Corp. 1982.

Acknowledgments

I would like to take this opportunity to thank the National Association of Buckskinners for their help and support. Also the Slonaker family—Butch, Dena ("Sunshine") and their son Charlie ("Sleeps in Fire")—whose friendship and warmth made this book so enjoyable to work on. I also want to thank Ron Price ("Possum") for his time and insight into modern-day rendezvous. I want to thank Barbara Peterson for her suggestions and ideas. To my editor and friend Rob Reilly, I can't thank you enough for your help and support. Finally, a special thanks to Ray and Linda Glazner for their time and valuable historical knowledge of the Fur Trade Era.

—K.R.

For More Information

The National Association of Buckskinners
P.O. Box 29307
Thornton, CO 80229

National Muzzle Loading Rifle Association
P.O. Box 67
Friendship, IN 47021
(812) 667-5131, (800) 745-1493

Credits

Text, captions and photographs ©1995 by Kurt Rhody
Foreword ©1995 by Ray Glazner
Text Editor: Rob Reilly
Book Design: Jeff Nicholas
Photo Editor: Jeff Nicholas
Printing coordinated by TWP, Ltd., Berkeley, CA
Printed in Singapore.
First printing: Spring 1996.

If you would like to receive
a complimentary catalog of publications
produced by Sierra Press—
please call:
1-800-745-2631
or write:
SIERRA PRESS, INC.
4988 Gold Leaf Drive
Mariposa, CA 95338